C000151966

Insults and Come-backs

Lines for All Occasions

KNOCK KNOCK®

LOS ANGELES, CALIFORNIA

Created and published by Knock Knock
6695 Green Valley Circle, #5167
Culver City, CA 90230
knockknockstuff.com

ISBN: 978-1-68349-259-7
UPC: 825703-50123-0

20 19 18 17 16 15 14 13 12 11 10 9 8 7 6 5 4

Contents

Intro

Preparing to Unleash the Beast

Whether you're teeming with frustration, overwhelmed with envy, or just plain in the mood, there are unlimited reasons to fire off an insult. From four-letter words to long-winded diatribes, backhanded compliments to in-your-face jeers, sometimes you've got to say what's really on your mind. The personal benefits of releasing such negative energy far outweigh someone else's hurt feelings. You'll feel empowered, in control, and generally better about yourself by taking down those around you. In today's world, niceness is overrated.

The pleasure of a skillfully delivered insult—and the frequently ensuing amusement—comes from the enjoyment of contrasting our own superiority with the foibles of others. Taking the comedic and insulting upper hand is an age-old form of dominance, and whether you are an insult's progenitor or have occasion to return one with a stinging comeback, delivering the right zingers will keep you at the top of the power hierarchy.

Your truth-telling statements may sting, but they also might do their recipients a favor, perhaps even inspiring a life change—a haircut, a trip to the library, or some serious counseling. We're surrounded by the ugly and the smelly, the crotchety and the immature, the stupid and the pretentious, and someone's got to take the initiative to tell it like it is.

If you're at a loss for what to insult, just remember the theory of relativity. If they're stupider than you, pick on their intelligence. If they're smarter, mock their arrogance. If they're mean, dis their character. If, on the other hand, you find yourself at the receiving end of a disparaging remark, you'll find the chapter on comebacks useful, an array of witty ripostes for every occasion.

When constructing barbs, think about the lines that best reflect your personality, intention, and desired outcome. Direct or slow-burning? Humorous or heinous? Ending or provoking a battle? Also consider your relationship to the insultee and the severity of the offense. Are you faced with an obnoxious driver, a reckless asshole with no regard for others? Or are you combating a friend who desperately needs encouragement to get in the shower? In addition, be sure to plan your delivery. Panache and confidence will help take the wind out of your opponents and garner the respect and admiration of others. Finally, whatever your purpose, always be sure to get in the last word.

Insults and Comebacks for All Occasions is here to make you witty AF and cement your superiority. By attacking those who need to be knocked down a peg, you'll make the world a better place one moron at a time. Bring it on!

Looks

**WHEN IT'S
ONLY SKIN DEEP**

DESPITE THE AGE-OLD SAYING THAT "WORDS will never hurt me," we all know that a biting comment can be a devastatingly effective slap in the face. And in today's looks-driven society, attacking people for superficial characteristics is one of the most effective ways to deliver a painful insult. What's the worst thing you can say to somebody these days? It's not telling them that they're unkind or lack integrity—it's "Your personal brand sucks."

If you have difficulty coming to terms with your desire to condemn someone's appearance, remember that the ugly among us are polluting our environment with their toxic looks and smells—whether they are Botox victims, hot messes, mullet lovers, unhygienic, or out of style. The $500+ billion-a-year global industry catering to looks—from makeup to cosmetic surgery—confirms how forceful these insults will be.

You can also pat yourself on the back for simultaneously putting someone down and accomplishing a greater good. If a friend has spinach in her teeth, you tell her, saving her from further embarrassment. The same is true if she has camel toe. The sooner you inform her of her flaw, the sooner

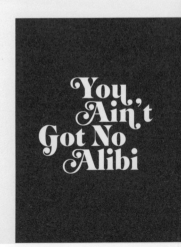

You, Ain't Got No Alibi

she can fix it—and that's one fewer visible (or odoriferous) offense in this world.

Calling out visual atrocities, aesthetic assaults, and fashion crimes is your civic duty and one way to make the world a little less ugly. Literally. And don't hold back if you have physical imperfections, but do brush up on your comebacks—just in case. Whether or not you're supermodel caliber, the beauty of a looks-based attack is not only its efficacy, it's also the self-esteem boost that comes from taking someone down because they're different from you.

~

Use caution when insulting an employee's appearance. Policies citing "community standards" of attractiveness have long been legally tolerated. However, in 2005, as part of the *Yanowitz v. L'Oréal* decision, the California Supreme Court ruled that "[Firing] a female employee for failing to meet a male executive's personal standards for sexual desirability is sex discrimination." Avoid statements such as the L'Oréal man's demand: "Get me somebody hot."

APPEARANCE

Oh, my God!
You look terrible.
Have you been sick?

~

Your face was
made for radio.

~

You're dark
and handsome.
When it's dark,
you're handsome.

~

Obviously, you
don't have any
fucks left to give.

~

Good for you for
giving conventional
beauty standards the
finger with your face!

I've had a
lot to drink,
and you still
don't look good.

~

Do you have to pay
extra for those
under-eye bags
when you fly?

~

A good plastic
surgeon could
fix that.

~

It's too bad your hot
body doesn't make
up for that nose.

~

Wow. You look
exhausted.

Ah, I understand—
you fell out of the
ugly tree and hit
every branch on
the way down.

❧

Can I borrow
your face for a few
days? My ass is
going on holiday.

❧

You've got
that faraway
look. The farther
away I get, the
better you look.

❧

There aren't
enough Snapchat
filters in the world
to make you look
cute. #facts

Let me guess:
you're the kid who
made a silly face and
it stayed that way.

❧

Kudos! It takes guts
to leave the house
looking like that.

❧

You have such
great hair.

❧

You have
such a great
personality.

❧

You're as pretty
as a picture—I
believe it's called
"The Scream."

SIZE & SHAPE

Clearly exercise isn't your thing.

&

Go ahead and pull up a sofa.

&

Now that food has replaced sex in your life, you can't even get into your own pants.

&

You must have to roll over more than a few times to get an even tan.

&

Your couch must be sick of your ass.

I remember you when you only had one chin.

&

You may not be good at losing weight, but you seem to be pretty good at finding it.

&

Evidently, you're an "inside person."

Ugly: The New Pretty

I bet your picture is
under the definition
of "gym rat" in
the dictionary.

That color really
complements your
stretch marks.

Lycra really
should come with
a warning label.

I feel honored
to have witnessed
your continual
growth.

Have you tried
celery juice?
I hear it helps
with bloating.

Just wondering
what those big
muscles are
compensating for.

If you want to insult someone by targeting their looks,
determine first whether you're addressing an ugliness
competitor; if so, you may not cause offense. Annual
contests for ugliest dog and homeliest baby draw large
numbers of contestants eager for fame and cash prizes.
In 2003, China held a Miss Ugly pageant one week
before hosting the Miss World competition. In addition
to the coveted title, the winner received $16,000 worth
of plastic surgery.

As a matter of fact, you do look fat in those pants.

I've never been attracted to the twelve-year-old-boy look.

❧

Your favorite food must be seconds.

For God's sake, eat a sandwich.

❧

I'd like to tell you about a little something we call a gym.

You put the "mean" in "lean and mean."

❧

Oh, I didn't see you—you were turned sideways.

Heroin chic is so last millennium.

❧

If you were drowning, I'd totally toss you a Cheerio.

Looks like your neck is trying to eat your face.

Did you ever
have boobs?

~

You must use a
Band-Aid as a maxi
pad and Chapstick
for deodorant.

~

Yellow makes
you look like a
no. 2 pencil.

~

You don't even
weigh enough
to give blood.

~

Your ensemble
does a terrific job
of maximizing
your flaws.

Whatever look
you were going
for, you missed.

~

What size is less
than zero?

~

It must be
comforting to know
there's a lid for every
jar—and a couch
for every potato.

STYLE

Did you dress
in the dark?

~

The '80s called—
they want their
wardrobe back.

I'm sure that would look good on someone.

~

You could be charged with excessive use of denim.

~

Very classy: visible thong and plumber's crack.

~

You look like shit. Is that the style now?

~

You look cheap—was that the point?

That top makes a statement. Too bad it's "fashion victim."

~

When you pull your pants up like that, I can see your manhood.

~

We've taken a vote: you're trying too hard.

Wolf in Sheep's Clothing

HYGIENE

Is that fabric
fire-retardant?

෴

Kudos on that
camel toe.

෴

Know where I can
score some coke?

෴

Hmm. That's an
interesting look.

I have two words
for you: personal
grooming.

෴

Just because
you can't smell it
doesn't mean the
rest of us aren't
suffering.

෴

Are you
going for the
hippie look?

Some of the most effective insults come in the form of backhanded compliments. The recipient will first be flattered, then insulted—a deft one-two punch. Comments such as "You've lost so much weight!" and "Your hair looks prettier today!" sound like praise, but the insult ("You looked so bad before!" and "Your hair usually looks awful!") lurks just below the surface. These Trojan horse insults appear harmless but will have the desired effect nonetheless.

Nice cologne. Must you marinate in it?

❧

May I offer you a mint?

❧

Do me a favor, and go through the car wash— without your car.

❧

It wouldn't be so bad if your personal scent wasn't so personal.

❧

Is it raining outside, or are you just really sweaty?

Actually, the unibrow look was never in.

❧

You have beautiful hair— coming from your nostrils and ears.

❧

Sorry, I just can't get past that giant zit on your forehead.

Tip: Insulting Gifts

I think there's
something living
in your beard.

Are you on
the European
laundry plan?

∾

∾

I never used to floss
until I realized
how much your
breath smelled.

May I suggest
some manscaping?

∾

∾

Are you French?

Your commitment
to not showering
is impressive.
And smelly.

∾

You smell like a
hard worker.

Not all insults are verbal. Why not present those
hygiene-challenged friends with a personal-care gift?
Subtle Butt is a disposable stick-on pad that neutralizes
flatulence. Ear Scope, a small camera, allows one to view
earwax excavation. For a more intimate insult, buy the
Weener Kleener, a donut-shaped personal soap product,
or the Biffy Squirt Travel Bidet. Finally, go mundane with
perfume, breath mints, or deodorant.

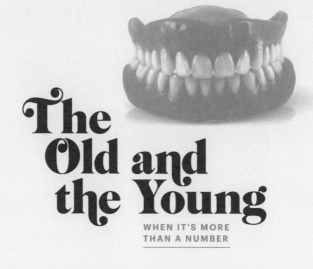

The Old and the Young

IN THE 2008 DOCUMENTARY film *The History of the Joke,* comedian Kathleen Madigan says audiences are almost always willing to accept jokes about age (vs. race or sex, for example). "For one thing, it's a common trait," states Madigan. "We're all going to get old sometime." The fact that there are always going to be elderly people around means that there's endless fodder for insults for the doddering. While perhaps the universality of the experience means the put-downs might be less painful than some of the other insult categories, they're still effective enough to keep in your arsenal of venom. Fortunately, culturally diminishing respect for elders means we're no longer socially prohibited from slamming seniors—whether for their aging minds, sagging bodies, or sad social lives.

It's also important to put uppity young 'uns in their place. Callow youth think they know everything. This is not only annoying, it's a cry for retribution. How else will the know-it-all young come to understand their ignorance and, most important, their place? Make sure these sophomoric upstarts realize the advan-

tages of your experience and wisdom and point out their naiveté at every opportunity.

Those who think young stay young at heart. What could keep you feeling more youthful than the smug satisfaction and gleeful hilarity that comes from insulting others for their chronological age, young or old?

∿

It used to be that elders were revered for their lifetime store of knowledge and wisdom. Fortunately, that's no longer the case, and old people are now acceptable targets for mockery. In explaining this shift, researchers have cited less traditional family structures, geographically spread-out families, popular culture's youth worship, parental indulgence, and generational selfishness. So, feel free to proceed with your ageist comments.

OBSOLETE

It's time to start
acting your age—old.

～

You're so old, you
think swiping is
something you
do on the toilet.

～

It may seem like
yesterday to you, but
it was decades ago.

～

You're so over
the hill, you
don't remember
crossing it.

～

You're so old,
you still think
Facebook is cool.

You're so old, you
call hashtags "the
pound sign."

～

Is your memory in
black and white?

～

You're so old, you
still get dressed
up when you fly.

～

You're so old, you
leave notes to remind
yourself to pee.

～

It must be hard
to be nostalgic
when you have
no memory of
your past.

You're so old,
you still end
sentences with
a period.

～

Yes, I've heard
that story before.
An hour ago.

～

You know so much.
Too bad you don't
remember anything.

～

Congratulations
on reaching your
second childhood!

～

You're so old,
you've got a @
yahoo account.

You're so old,
you print out
driving directions.

～

You're so old,
you still
carry cash.

～

You're so old, you
don't know how to
pronounce "meme."

～

You're so old,
you watch the
nightly news.

～

You're so old, you
think "thirsty"
means you need
some water.

You're so old,
you've never
googled yourself.

~

OK, boomer.

AGING BODIES

You're so old,
you fart dust.

~

For some people,
forty is the new
twenty-nine, but
I don't think you
can pull that off.

~

Does it take you
twice as long to
look half as good?

At least your
failing eyes will
keep you from
seeing the rest of
your failing body.

~

It may be too
late for Botox.

~

It takes you
longer to rest
than it did to
get tired.

Youth: Wasted on the Old

The only thing you
should exercise
is caution.

Poor thing—
wrinkles and acne!

What's left
of your hair is
getting so gray!

What a double
whammy to
say goodbye to
both your hipness
and your hip.

The good news
is you look like
you should be
respected; the bad
news is you're not.

You remember
when phones
hung on the wall.

The booming youth-maintenance market is a testament
of age insults. If aging weren't a sensitive topic, the
United States wouldn't have logged close to 18 million
cosmetic procedures in 2018, with Botox leading the
way. If you believe the pharmaceutical commercials,
as many as 30 million older American men suffer from
erectile dysfunction. When people freeze their faces and
their penises to freeze time, there's plenty to laugh at
them about.

DINOSAURS

Your social
security number
must be in the
single digits.

~

They've asked you
to be on *Antiques
Roadshow*—
to be appraised.

~

I wish I'd known
you when you
were alive.

~

When you were
born, the Dead Sea
was just sick.

~

Weren't you a waiter
at the Last Supper?

Did you have a pet
dinosaur when
you were a kid?

~

You're so old, the
candles cost more
than the cake.

~

When you
were in school,
history was called
"current events."

~

When you were in
school, evolution
hadn't happened yet.

~

If I told you
to act your age,
you'd die.

NO GAME

I was at the
ancient history
museum today and
thought of you.

The only time you
hear heavy breathing
is during a cardiac
stress test.

✌

✌

I bet you think
the '90s
weren't that
long ago.

You're so old, you
think "Netflix
and chill" involves
actually watching
something.

✌

✌

It must get
heavy carrying
around that
generation gap.

That menoPorsche
is such a cliché.

✌

✌

If this is your
midlife crisis,
I guess you're
planning to
live to 120 or
something?

Your idea of happy
hour is a nap.

✌

Do you burn the
midnight oil
until 9 PM?

When you're on vacation, your energy runs out before your money does.

❧

Now that you're old enough to watch your step, you're too old to go anywhere.

❧

You're so old, you've never been ghosted.

❧

You're so old, your idea of oral sex is talking about it.

❧

You can't get it up—you can't even get up.

I'd ask you to go upstairs and make love to me, but I don't think you're young enough to do either.

❧

You still read the newspaper.

❧

At your age, "getting lucky" means finding your car in the parking lot.

Fight the Power

You get tired
wrestling with
temptation.

You still think
you can be
anything you
want—and get
paid for it.

CALLOW
YOUTH

You remind me of
when I was young
and clueless.

You still think
you'll have that
body forever.

~

~

You think you
deserve a trophy
just for being born.

You still think the
world owes you.

By preparing yourself to taunt the elderly, you're
planning for the future. Thanks to the large baby boomer
population and increased life expectancy, the number of
maturing seniors (age 55 and older) in the United States
is expected to top 1 billion by 2030. Given that this
expanding demographic will strain the economy and
families alike, the insults will be well deserved indeed.

You still think you
can have it all.

∽

You still think
you can change
the world.

∽

You still think
you're hot shit.

∽

You still think
your dreams will
come true.

∽

You're so young,
you think people
other than your
parents will believe
you're talented.

You actually
believe you're
special.

∽

Have some
more $8
avocado toast.

∽

You're so young,
you think you
deserve promotions
and raises without
hard work.

Tip:
Don't
Give
Them
Tips

I bet you took a selfie as you slid out of the womb.

❧

Your lack of experience is matched only by your surplus of ego.

❧

Your youthful idealism makes me want to puke.

You still think you know everything.

❧

You should have grown out of that by now.

❧

Just keep scrolling, just keep scrolling.

❧

Grow up!

It's easy to get irritated when talking to the young: they're naive, immature, idealistic know-it-alls. Don't ever try to share your wisdom; they'll never grasp it, and their quick wit may get the best of you, as in this fifth-century-BC exchange between uncle and nephew:

> Pericles: "When I was your age, Alcibiades, I talked just the way you are now talking."

> Alcibiades: "If only I had known you, Pericles, when you were at your best."

Brains

**WHEN THEY JUST
DON'T GET IT**

YOU'VE ALREADY PROVEN YOUR intelligence by choosing to utilize this compendium of insults. Now, it's time to take down the lesser beings around you. Whether they're dumber than a doorknob, emotionally challenged, or even too smart for their own good, you shouldn't have to put up with their idiocy, because you now have the skill and wit to put them in their place.

Morons lurk everywhere. Idiot drivers, incompetent coworkers, basket-case friends, socially inept experts—you are surrounded. And no doubt you're sick of it. Your victim's level of intelligence or education is actually immaterial, because your insult will be a reaction to an unbelievably imbecilic moment or to your target's overall ineptitude.

For those who are truly stupid, keep it simple. If they're not book smart, prey on their insecurities by using big words. For the talent-free, let them know that their cooking sucks, they can't write, or they're just plain mediocre. If they're emotionally weak-minded—those who may seem otherwise intelligent but who fall

Survival
of the
Fittest

again and again into destructive patterns—be sure to point this out when it arises. Finally, a smarty-pants is just as annoying as a dimwit. Remember that "pretentious" comes from the root for "pretend": these blowhards need to be taken down, their bombast exposed.

With this book, you've got the smarts to combat both boneheads and braggarts. Get out there and cut them off at the knees.

&

The Darwin Awards recognize and commemorate those whose extreme stupidity kills them, thus removing them from the gene pool. One award winner, a farmer from Poland, chopped off his own head with a chain saw during a drunken game of macho one-upmanship. Two college students were recognized for crawling into a giant helium advertising balloon to get high; due to their failure to remember the human need for oxygen, they suffocated.

DIM BULBS

I wish I were as
smart as you
think you are.

~

If you can't
pronounce it,
don't say it.

~

I'm sorry—I didn't
mean to use so
many syllables.

~

Really? You "could
care less"?

~

Good thing you're
not letting your
education get in
the way of your
ignorance.

The fact that no
one understands
you doesn't mean
you're an artist.

~

Where'd you hear
that—on Twitter?

~

You really earned
that BS degree,
didn't you?

~

Don't let the facts
get in the way of
your opinions.

~

Critical thinking—
it's a thing. You
should try it
sometime.

Congratulations on
barely graduating.

～

Spell-check was
invented for
people like you.

～

You should get a
refund on that
college education.

～

I'd like to insult
you, but you
wouldn't get it.

JUST PLAIN STUPID

Even your "street
smarts" are dumb.

I don't know what
makes you so dumb,
but it really works.

～

If brains were
taxed, you'd
get a rebate.

～

If you spoke your
mind, you'd be
speechless.

～

Don't get lost
in thought—it's
unfamiliar territory.

～

Don't let your
mind wander—
it's too little to be
let out alone.

You're so dumb,
blondes tell jokes
about you.

～

You're so dumb,
your dog teaches
you tricks.

～

You're so dumb,
you sold your car
for gas money.

～

You're so dumb,
you think a lawsuit
is something you
wear to court.

～

It's a good thing
you're cute.

I smell something
burning. Oh wait,
that's just your brain
trying to work.

～

Brains aren't
everything. In
fact, in your case
they're nothing.

～

You'd need twice
as much sense to
be a half-wit.

Dumb to the Roots

If what you don't know can't hurt you, you're practically invulnerable.

❧

I hope your smart phone is extra-smart to make up for all your stupid.

❧

Most people live and learn. You just live.

You're undisputable proof that common sense isn't very common.

❧

❧

You put the "less" in "witless."

Ignorance can be cured. Stupid is forever.

The time-honored "dumb blonde" joke dates to the 1925 publication of Anita Loos's novel *Gentlemen Prefer Blondes*. The book showcased Lorelei Lee, a ditzy, gold-digging blonde—who was actually pretty smart. After a lesser-known 1928 film version, Lorelei was, of course, famously played by Marilyn Monroe in 1953.

INEPT

FYI, there's this magical thing called a dictionary. Look it up.

～

Your mediocrity is unparalleled.

～

Oh, I'm sorry—I didn't realize I was supposed to laugh.

～

For some, following a recipe is just hard.

～

One of the defining characteristics of writers is the fact that they write.

It's not the technology—it's you.

～

Talking about it and doing it are two very different things. At least you excel at something: talking about it.

～

You're the only one who believes in your talent.

～

It takes a special skill set to be as clueless as you are.

～

Don't quit your day job.

If you're playing dumb, you're really good at it.

ONE SHORT, TWO SHY

You're one banana short of a fruit salad.

❧

You're one sentence short of a paragraph.

❧

You're two sheep shy of a sweater.

❧

You're a couple of knights shy of a Crusade.

You're a few beers short of a six-pack.

❧

You're a few birds shy of a flock.

❧

You're a few clowns short of a circus.

❧

You're a few Bradys short of a bunch.

❧

You're a few eggs short of a dozen.

❧

You're a few Skittles® short of a rainbow.

BRAINS

You're a few peas short of a pod.

You're a few rungs short of a ladder.

You're a few french fries short of a Happy Meal.

You're a few sandwiches short of a picnic.

LOW EQ

There's no trophy for always being the last one at the party.

Baggage is one thing; steamer trunks are another.

If you pay attention, you can tell when people aren't interested in what you have to say.

Let me guess, you're in love—again.

Stupid Quotes

When something happens to you over and over again, what do you think is the common denominator?

∽

You would think being married four times was enough.

∽

What did you expect?

Spoiler alert! The world doesn't actually revolve around you.

∽

There's this thing called an inside voice. Ever heard of it?

∽

Get a hold of yourself.

"Common sense is not so common." —Voltaire

"Stupidity is the same as evil if you judge by the results." —Margaret Atwood

"Many people would sooner die than think. In fact, they do." —Bertrand Russell

"Beauty fades, dumb is forever." —Judge Judy Sheindlin

BRAINS

You're smart, funny, and pretty, and you have terrible taste in men.

*

You're smart, funny, and handsome, and you have terrible taste in women.

*

Can't you see the pattern here?

SMARTY-PANTS

You're just not user-friendly.

*

It's lonely at the top, isn't it?

If you were as smart as you think you are, you'd realize you come off like a pretentious asshole.

*

Peppering your speech with foreign phrases does not endear you to others.

*

My god, you're boring.

Slang Slams

Why don't you just join Mensa and call it a day?

~

Making other people feel stupid doesn't make you seem smarter.

~

Yes, you have a huge vocabulary, but what good is it if no one understands you?

~

Clearly you've chosen knowing everything over having friends.

~

You're what they call "book smart," and not in a good way.

~

Differential equations just aren't sexy.

Basic = mainstream, unoriginal
Bye, Felicia = go away, you're dismissed
Clap back = witty comeback or zinger
Extra = over the top, dramatic AF
Ratchet = trashy, rude
Read = catty put-down, savage insult
Sus = suspicious, shady
Salty = acting bitter or upset
Thirsty = hungry for approval and/or attention
Throwing shade = subtle trash-talking

Character

WHEN WE CONTEMPLATE CHARACTER, WE think of traits such as morality, integrity, humaneness, maturity, honesty, and kindness. As evidenced by chapter 1, our society values beauty and celebrity far more than the deeper virtues, but there's still much to target in a character-based attack. And with fewer people exhibiting sound character these days, there are plenty of individuals for whom these insults will prove handy.

It is said that the flaws we hate the most in others are the flaws we ourselves possess, so go right ahead and condemn people for things you yourself do. If you are any of the types addressed in this chapter—assholes, bitches, egotists, attitude givers, nutjobs, freaks, liars, cheats, sluts, man-whores, losers, and bores—your vast insight will give you a clear path to takedown.

If you're a decent, ethical person, you'll need this chapter's guidance all the more, because your moral compass won't allow you to come up with appropriate attacks. While you may feel initially guilty about

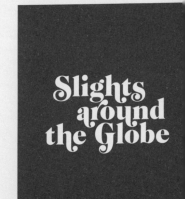

Slights around the Globe

going on the offensive, be confident in your approach and message—chances are you're not the only one your target aggravates.

Whether you are a good or bad person, if you encounter someone with multiple contemptible characteristics, go for the combo approach: choose insults from the various categories to concoct a nuclear affront, then rest assured that the world will be grateful.

∾

Slandering someone's brains or personality isn't always the most effective mode of insult, especially abroad. In Italy and Latin America, the surest means of offense is trashing a person's mother, while Dutch natives sometimes mention disease or disability in their slams. In Arab regions, exposing the sole of your shoe is as offensive as it gets, while in East Asia, touching or patting someone on the head does the trick.

ASSHOLES

If I wanted to hear from an asshole, I'd fart.

❧

I'd tell you to eat a giant bag of dicks, but you obviously already had one for breakfast.

❧

Do you have to work that hard to be a jerk, or does it just come naturally?

❧

You used to be arrogant and obnoxious. Now you're the opposite— obnoxious and arrogant.

You're not yourself today! I noticed the improvement immediately.

❧

You're not hot enough to be such a douche.

❧

Jesus told me he thinks you're a jerk.

❧

See you next Tuesday.

❧

I don't think you're an asshole, but I seem to be in the minority.

When people say you're the perfect jerk, I tell them you're not perfect, but you're doing all right.

～

You're not even *beneath* my contempt.

～

You're the reason God created the middle finger.

～

Your father should have pulled out.

～

You put the "turd" in Saturday.

Men have that time of the month, too.

～

You have a real knack for making people hate you.

～

You should come with a warning label.

EGOS AND ATTITUDES

I know you're self-made. It's big of you to take the blame!

～

It's hard to get over yourself, isn't it?

Jesus may love you, but everybody else thinks you're an ass.

~

I bet that attitude of yours was *really* cool back in high school.

~

There might be two sides to every story, but you're still delusional in both of them.

~

I'm impressed. I've never met someone with such a small mind inside such a big head before.

There's Mr. Right, there's Mr. Wrong, and then there's you—Mr. Never Wrong.

~

What exactly does your big head compensate for?

~

Your ego is sucking all the oxygen out of the room.

Silent but Deadly

Yes, the cream rises to the top, but so does the scum.

It'll be a lonely day when all you have to keep you company is your own ego.

~

Are you still paying off your student loans to poseur school?

HEAD CASES

I'm guessing you haven't been diagnosed yet.

~

I'm not sure how we'd manage to live without you, but I'm sure it'd be awesome.

~

Who am I talking to today?

Anthropologists estimate that over 90 percent of communication is nonverbal. Whatever the situation, the lines in this book can, therefore, take you only so far. For example, if you want to ding someone lightly, smile when you deliver your insult. If the infraction is dire, roll your eyes and snort in disgust. Stand-alone signs such as the middle finger, up yours (fist to upward-bending inner elbow), or chin flick will always help you get the last nonword in.

Your personality's
split so many ways
you go alone for
group therapy.

❧

You might want to
go back home to
take your meds.

❧

Have you thought
about upping
the dosage?

❧

It's supposed to be
better living through
modern chemistry.

❧

I've read about
people like you in my
Psych 101 textbook.

Your mind isn't
just twisted—
it's sprained.

❧

As an outsider,
what do you think
of the human race?

❧

You're not even
half-baked—you're
just plain raw.

❧

You must have
gotten up on the
wrong side of
the padded room
this morning.

❧

What's it like being
dead inside?

I'd suggest therapy, but there's no cure for narcissism.

❧

I bet your therapist is publishing a paper on you.

❧

Your baggage is so heavy you can't even lug it onto the couch.

❧

You put the *psycho* in *psychology*.

LIARS AND CHEATS

You're as good as your word, and your vocabulary sucks.

You'd make a great politician.

❧

Roses are red, violets are blue, I've got five fingers and the middle one's for you.

❧

While you're stabbing my back, feel free to kiss my ass.

❧

Calling you a dirty liar would be an insult to dirty liars.

❧

Tomorrow is trash pickup. Hope you've got your bags packed.

You're so dishonest,
I can't even be
sure that what you
tell me are lies.

≈

Does the smell of
the shit coming
out of your mouth
make you wanna
vomit too?

≈

Thanks for your
outstanding
portrayal of the
Biggest Dick Ever in
the story of my life.

≈

Death wouldn't
be that big of
a deal for you—
either way,
you're lying.

I didn't get why they
called it the rat race
until I met you.

≈

Your motto is
if two wrongs
don't make a right,
try a third.

≈

Not even your
dog thinks you're
a good person.

**Tip:
Gas-
lighting**

I'm surprised
you can see past
those dollar signs
in your eyes.

I can always tell
when you're lying.
Your lips move.

❧

You lie like a rug.

You must get lots
of exercise talking
out of both sides
of your mouth.

❧

The only difference
between you and a
mosquito is that one
is a bloodsucking
parasite and the
other is an insect.

❧

Even if you make
yourself believe
it, it's still a lie.

When dealing with someone who's a little loony, don't just call him crazy—make him crazy, then follow up by insulting his sanity. The classic 1944 thriller *Gaslight* depicts a woman tricked into thinking she's going mad. Her husband moves objects and dims the gaslights and then denies that anything is happening—hence the term "gaslight," to manipulate someone's perceptions so she will believe she's losing her mind.

LOSERS

Your inferiority complex is fully justified.

You're one bad relationship away from having thirty cats.

Anyone who told you to be yourself couldn't have given you worse advice.

You remind me of one of those people in school that no one remembers.

I'm swiping left on this conversation. Bye!

You bore me, and I even enjoy watching paint dry.

You're better than Ambien, and cheaper.

Specific Neologisms

I'm trying to imagine you with a personality.

I've had three triple-shot expressos and you're still making me feel like I need a nap.

≈

You're such a loser, your imaginary friends wouldn't hang out with you.

≈

Googling you yielded no results.

You're so boring, you can't even entertain a doubt.

≈

You're such a loser, when someone tells you to get a life, you ask, "Where?"

≈

There must be *something* interesting about you.

Certain put-downs are originated by particular groups to describe unique situations. Some favorites: seagull manager (a bureaucrat who flies in, makes a lot of noise, craps all over everything, and leaves), Velcroid (someone who shadows a celebrity in order to get into photos), 404 (clueless, from the HTML error message "404 error: File not found"), and whorganic (of or pertaining to the naturally whorish). The possibilities are endless!

Counter-attacks

IT'S A SAD REALITY OF LIFE THAT YOU WON'T always be the one delivering the insult— sometimes others will attack you. Since you don't know when or from where such an assault will occur, you'll want to be sure your defensive game is buttoned up. As you insult more frequently, others will begin to admire your clever zingers. They'll turn on you quickly, and you'd better be ready with as much wit in the return as in the serve.

Depending on your relationship with the attacker and the manner in which they attack, there are many ways to craft your response. In some instances, you'll simply want to call upon a classic—short, sharp, and direct. You can select one that's dismissive, suggesting that they are so not worth your time, or one that's potentially duel inciting, in which case you'll emerge as the silver-tongued victor.

For a particularly mean insult, you'll want to have an equally cutting reply. For complete idiots or the utterly demented, make sure your retort expresses just how unoriginal or nonsensical your attackers are. Or, when you've simply had enough, unleash an end-all line that will shut them up for good.

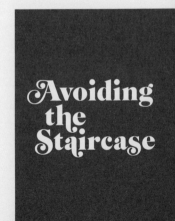

Avoiding
the
Staircase

Rehearse these lines so you'll be ready for any barb hurled your way—no momentum-killing pause, no stumbling over your words, no thinking of the perfect comeback hours too late. This is your moment to shine, when you can truly put your skills to the test and leave others in your comeback wake.

～

The French expression *l'esprit de l'escalier* means "the wit of the staircase": the devastatingly witty comeback concocted after the confrontation, too late to deliver, on the way down the staircase. Germans have coined a similar term: *treppenwitz* (*treppen* means "stairs," *witz* means "wit"). With practice and the lines in this chapter, your goal is to preempt the staircase, issuing your scathing ripostes on point and on time.

CLASSICS

Bite me!

∽

Bring it on!

∽

Oh, it's so on.

∽

Feel special now?

∽

It takes one to know one!

∽

Talk to the booty, 'cause the hand's off duty!

∽

Take a chill pill.

Up your nose with a rubber hose.

∽

Talk to the hand.

∽

That's not what your mother said last night.

∽

Whatever.

∽

As if!

∽

Am not!

∽

Piss off.

I know you are,
but what am I?

Thank you for
sharing.

&

&

Liar, liar, pants
on fire!

Sticks and
stones may
break my bones,
but words will
never hurt me.

&

Get a life!

&

&

Up yours!

Shut your
pie hole!

&

&

Take a long walk
off a short pier.

Bye, Felicia!

&

&

Yo' mama.

I'm rubber,
you're glue;
whatever you say
bounces off me
and sticks to you.

&

So there.

BULLIES

It's clear from
your behavior
that you must have
had a miserable
childhood.

∾

A sharp tongue
is no indication
of a keen mind.

∾

You put the "ass"
in "asshole."

∾

Did your mother
teach you to treat
people like that?

∾

Let's switch places:
you be funny, and
I'll be an asshole.

I will always
cherish the initial
misconceptions I
had about you.

∾

I'm only interested
in the opinions of
people I respect.

∾

I may be fat,
but you're ugly,
and I can
always diet.

Yo'
Mama

People treat others the way they feel about themselves—it must be hard to be you.

I may be ignorant, but you're stupid, and I can always study.

❧

I may be immature, but you're old, and I can always grow up.

Someday you'll find out the truth: karma's a bitch.

❧

When you go to hell, you're going to lower the property values.

You don't want to blow a gasket, because I'm not a mechanic.

Also known as *the dozens*, *capping*, and *dissing*, "yo' mama" has evolved into a call-and-response competitive art form. Insult matches date at least to the eighth century, when Arab poets traded barbs in the town square, collected as *Al-Naqa'id*. And in the Middle Ages, Scots verbally abused one another in flyting contests. Today, "mama" insults target obesity, appearance, and stupidity. As a comeback, simply replying "Yo' mama" is a classic.

Careful, there—if the redness in your face is any indication, your blood pressure's on the rise.

⌇

Wow, you're as mean as everybody says you are.

RESPONDING TO IDIOTS

Wow, it must have hurt when your daddy dropped you.

⌇

The next time I need an unsolicited and uninformed opinion, I'll know where to go.

Did you eat lots of paste as a kid?

⌇

Shall I speak slower?

⌇

Does your stream of consciousness have any fish in it?

⌇

I can see your point, but I still think you're an idiot.

⌇

What the actual fuck?

⌇

That insult is staler than your breath.

That insult was out of date when Adam used it on Eve.

❧

It must be nice to be free of the burden of intelligence.

❧

If I agreed with you, we'd both be wrong.

❧

You have nothing to say, but you say it so loudly.

❧

Your lips are moving, but nothing's coming out.

I'm sorry, I don't speak "Stupid."

❧

I'm blonde. What's your excuse?

DISSING DYSFUNCTION

Are you in therapy for that?

❧

You might want to cut back on the sugar.

❧

It's nice to meet an alcoholic who doesn't want to remain anonymous.

I'm sorry,
I don't speak
in tongues.

❧

You're gonna
need a bigger
boat for all your
baggage.

❧

I don't know
what your
problem is, but
I'll bet it's hard
to pronounce.

❧

I see you've
set aside this
special time to
humiliate yourself
in public.

Cancel my
subscription—
I can't deal with
your issues.

❧

Did you not get
enough attention
at home?

❧

Any resemblance
between your reality
and mine is strictly
coincidental.

**Foreign
Tongue
Lashings**

They have a special place for people like you.

~

Are you high?

~

Are you for real?

SHUTTING THEM UP

You're canceled.

How about a little less talk and a little more shut-the-hell-up?

~

I don't mind your talking as long as you don't mind my not listening.

~

I don't like you—and I always will.

When responding to an insult from an idiot, try using another language to make your opponent feel even more stupid than he or she may actually be. Try "idiot" in Finnish (*tampio*), Portuguese (*abestado*), Hawaiian (*hupo*), Tagalog (*tanga*), or French (*connard*). Consult translation dictionaries for more variations on the theme, or use sign language: make a fist and strike your forehead as though knocking sense into it.

Do us all a favor
and go away.

～

Is that the best
you've got?

～

I'm busy now. Can
I ignore you some
other time?

～

There's a game you
might enjoy: it's
called hide and go
screw yourself.

～

I don't mind your
talking as long as
you don't mind my
not listening.

Don't bother me;
I'm living happily
ever after.

～

I'd like to help
you out. Which
way did you
come in?

～

You've obviously
mistaken me for
someone who
gives a shit.

Tip: Crafting Comebacks

If I promise to
miss you, will
you go away?

Buuuh-bye.

❧

❧

Delete your account.

Why are you
even talking?

❧

❧

Thank U, next.

If you were roadkill,
not even the vultures
would eat you.

❧

❧

Why don't you
go out and play
with the buses.

We're done here.

To deliver stellar comebacks, take a few pointers from
improv performers, for whom a classic pitfall is thinking
about their response rather than listening to their part-
ners. Until it's time for you to reply, focus carefully on
your opponent's words. Then come from a place of "Yes,
and . . ." rather than "No, but . . ." to help your verbal
flexibility. The skill of the comeback is akin to martial
arts—you must stay in the moment and play off your
opponent's moves.

COUNTERATTACKS

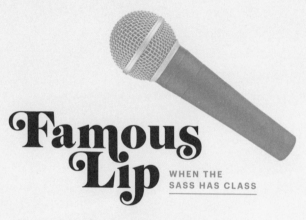

Famous Lip

WHEN THE
SASS HAS CLASS

INSULTS AREN'T LIMITED TO LAY PEOPLE.
Well-known actors, artists, writers, musicians, and politicians are also deep in the game. Part of the reason for their success is that they know half of looking good is making others look bad. For some, publicly documented insults were their original claims to fame.

Where the previous chapters provided actual verbiage for your everyday usage, here you will find inspiration for the inevitable moments when you need to go off-script. At this point in the book, you should have a fairly solid grasp of what lines to use when. Now that you're at least at the intermediate level, you'll be even more impressed at the verbal acuity of insults that have stood the test of time. Indeed, perhaps the most acclaimed lines aren't insults, but comebacks, as celebrities who are able to turn an attack into an even better affront garner the most respect and admiration.

Hopefully this book has piqued your interest in the insult and comeback arts. If you want to go further for inspiration, investigate the words of such greats as Oscar Wilde, Groucho

The Insult Barb

Marx, Dorothy Parker, and Mark Twain. With a little practice, you too may be able to conjure up insults so perfect, so apropos, so witty, that they live on forever not only in the hearts and minds of those who were lucky enough to have heard them, but on the written page as an example of the best of the best.

〜

Among other things, William Shakespeare has gone down in history as creator of the most original insults ever written. Try an easy-to-follow method to craft your own: first, choose a degrading adjective; next, a hyphenated, verb-derived adjective; and finally, link them with a rich noun (for example, *dumpy* plus *addle-brained* plus *fop*). Or, use a direct quote from the master (say, "poisonous bunch-back'd toad").

SMARTS

"He's a nice guy, but he played too much football with his helmet off."
—Lyndon B. Johnson, on Gerald Ford

~

"He is not a free thinker. He is a free moron who doesn't read."
—Roxane Gay, on Kanye West

~

"It's a new low for actresses when you have to wonder what's between her ears instead of her legs." —Katharine Hepburn, on Sharon Stone

"He had a mind so fine that no idea could violate it."
—T. S. Eliot, on Henry James

~

"I'll explain and I'll use small words so that you'll be sure to understand, you warthog-faced buffoon."
—Westley to Prince Humperdinck (*The Princess Bride*)

~

"He can compress the most words into the smallest idea of any man I know."
—Abraham Lincoln, target unknown

CHARACTER

Why, you stuck-up, half-witted, scruffy-looking nerf-herder! — Princess Leia to Han Solo (*The Empire Strikes Back*)

✎

"Sarah Palin met with world leaders to discuss her foreign policy expertise. The meeting lasted 90 seconds." —Conan O'Brien, on Sarah Palin

✎

"If he were any dumber, he'd be a tree."—Barry Goldwater, on William Scott

I wonder whether Trump talks to Trumpself in the third Trumperson when Trump's alone. —J. K. Rowling (Twitter)

✎

"He's the type of man who will end up dying in his own arms." —Mamie Van Doren, on Warren Beatty

✎

Dear Shia Labeouf. It's getting creepy the fact that you can't stop talking about me. It's been 12 years now. I don't know you. Thanks. —Frankie Muniz (Twitter)

"If you gave Jerry Falwell an enema, you could bury him in a matchbox." —Christopher Hitchens, on Jerry Falwell

"If they can make penicillin out of moldy bread, they can sure make something out of you." —Muhammad Ali, to a young boxer

"I loathe you. You revolt me stewing in your consumption . . . you are a loathsome reptile— I hope you die." —D. H. Lawrence, to Katherine Mansfield

"What other problems do you have besides being unemployed, a moron, and a dork?" —John McEnroe, to a tennis spectator

"Always willing to lend a helping hand to the one above him." —F. Scott Fitzgerald, on Ernest Hemingway

Music Digs

"Good taste would likely have the same effect on Howard Stern that daylight has on Dracula."
—Ted Koppel

"He is the same old sausage, fizzing and sputtering in his own grease." —Henry James, on Thomas Carlyle

"I literally pose half naked for a living and u are still the biggest attention whore I know." —Chrissy Teigen, on Donald Trump (Twitter)

"He has no more backbone than a chocolate éclair." —Theodore Roosevelt, on William McKinley

Some of today's most quotable put-downs come from popular-music lyrics. Set your insult to a melody or beat and before long others will sing your slur. Here are some toe-tapping favorites:

"Every time I think of you, I puke." —Eminem

"Were you born an asshole, or did you work at it your whole life?" —Jimmy Buffett

"I'm so ugly, but that's okay, 'cause so are you." —Nirvana

"Idiot wind, blowing every time you move your mouth." —Bob Dylan

"For years I've regarded [his] very existence as a monument to all the rancid genes and broken chromosomes that corrupt the possibilities of the American Dream; he was a foul caricature of himself, a man with no soul, no inner convictions, with the integrity of a hyena and the style of a poison toad." —Hunter S. Thompson, on Richard Nixon

ص

"I like a drink as much as the next man. Unless the next man is Mel Gibson." —Ricky Gervais

"I knew her before she was a virgin." —Oscar Levant, on Doris Day

ص

"He is limp and damp and milder than the breath of a cow." —Virginia Woolf, on E. M. Forster

ص

"The man was a major comedian, which is to say that he had the compassion of an icicle, the effrontery of a carnival shill, and the generosity of a pawnbroker." —S. J. Perelman, on Groucho Marx

TALENT

"... a skillful but short-lived decorator."
—Edgar Degas, on Claude Monet

∾

"He bores me. He ought to have stuck to his flying machines."
—Auguste Renoir, on Leonardo da Vinci

∾

"A hack writer ... who tried out a few of the old proven 'sure-fire' literary skeletons with sufficient local color to intrigue the superficial and the lazy." —William Faulkner, on Mark Twain

"What's that? You want to know where I got my boots? They're from You Can't Afford Them and Stop Talking to Me."
—Amy Schumer, to a heckler

∾

"Michael Jackson's album was only called *Bad* because there wasn't enough room on the sleeve for *Pathetic*." —Prince

∾

"I have more talent in my smallest fart than you have in your entire body."
—Walter Matthau, to Barbra Streisand

#ThingsToNever-AskaDJ "Got any Backstreet Boys?? Bam." —Justin Timberlake (Twitter)

～

"He couldn't ad-lib a fart after a baked-bean dinner." —Johnny Carson, on Chevy Chase

～

"Wet, she's a star. Dry, she ain't." —Fanny Brice, on Esther Williams

～

"She ran the whole gamut of emotions from A to B." —Dorothy Parker, on Katharine Hepburn

"He writes his plays for the ages—the ages between five and twelve." —George Nathan, on George Bernard Shaw

～

"I have tried lately to read Shakespeare, and found it so intolerably dull that it nauseated me." —Charles Darwin

Tip:
Afix an
Epithet

"Her voice sounded like an eagle being goosed." —Ralph Novak, on Yoko Ono

"He is to acting what Liberace was to pumping iron." —Rex Reed, on Sylvester Stallone

"I don't know her." —Mariah Carey, on Jennifer Lopez

"I just heard Nick Cannon is starting a comedy tour. Who's going to do the comedy?" —Chelsea Handler (Twitter)

"That's not writing, that's typing." —Truman Capote, on Jack Kerouac

If you asked Typhoid Mary, Vlad the Impaler, or Ivan the Terrible, you'd learn that the unflattering epithet—permanently linked to one's name—is the ultimate form of offense. Many historic rulers have had to live down devastating sobriquets, such as Ethelred the Unready, Halfdan the Mild, Charles the Bald, and Ivailo the Cabbage. Come up with a descriptive epithet, repeat it frequently, and hope your enemy will be saddled with it forever!

TIT FOR TAT

Henry Clay: "I would rather be right than be president." Congressman Reed: "He doesn't have to worry. He'll never be either."

~

Lord Sandwich: "Really, Mr. Wilkes, I don't know whether you'll die on the gallows or of the pox." John Wilkes: "That will depend, my lord, on whether I embrace your principles or your mistress."

~

Noel Coward: "You look almost like a man." Edna Ferber: "So do you."

Old Spice (Twitter): "Why is it that 'fire sauce' isn't made with any real fire? Seems like false advertising." Taco Bell (Twitter): @OldSpice "Is your deodorant made with really old spices?"

~

Young man: "I can't bear fools." Dorothy Parker: "Apparently, your mother could."

Merchant of Venom

"I've been called worse things by better men." —Pierre Trudeau's response to learning that Richard Nixon had called him an asshole

Joe Frazier: "He's phony, using his blackness to get his way." Muhammad Ali: "Joe Frazier is so ugly he should donate his face to the U.S. Bureau of Wildlife."

෴

Nancy Astor: "Winston, if you were my husband, I'd put poison in your coffee." Winston Churchill: "Nancy, if you were my wife, I'd drink it."

෴

Clare Boothe Luce: "Age before beauty." Dorothy Parker: "Pearls before swine."

The comedian Don Rickles built his long career on the art of the insult. His equal-opportunity barbs (he mocks all races, lifestyles, and religions), honed against hecklers, skillfully manage to malign without being contemptuous. In 1957, he made his mark with Frank Sinatra, a notorious hothead, by saying, "Make yourself at home, Frank—hit somebody." Sinatra laughed, and celebrities kept lining up, hoping to be Rickles' next target, until his death in 2017.